Un Poco Loco

Other Collections by Richard Lyons

These Modern Nights, University of Missouri Press
Hours of the Cardinal, University of South Carolina Press
Fleur Carnivore, 2005 Washington Prize, Word Works

Un Poco Loco

poems

Richard Lyons

Iris Press
Oak Ridge, Tennessee

Cover photo:
52nd Street, New York, N.Y., ca. 1948
William P. Gottlieb Collection (DLC) 99-401005
Library of Congress

Frontispiece:
Portrait of Nat King Cole, New York, N.Y., ca. June 1947
William P. Gottlieb Collection (DLC) 99-401005
Library of Congress

Author photo: Megan Bean / Mississippi State University

Book design: Robert B. Cumming, Jr.

Library of Congress Cataloging-in-Publication Data

Names: Lyons, Richard, 1951- author.
Title: Un poco loco : poems / Richard Lyons.
Description: Oak Ridge, Tennessee : Iris Press, [2016] | Includes
   bibliographical references.
Identifiers: LCCN 2016010302 | ISBN 9781604542332 (pbk. : alk. paper)
Classification: LCC PS3562.Y4494 A6 2016 | DDC 811/.54—dc23
LC record available at http://lccn.loc.gov/2016010302

Acknowledgments

The Adroit Journal: "Talk about Crazy"

The Alaska Quarterly Review: "A Human Throat"

Brilliant Corners: "For Bud Powell: Un Poco Loco," "Blues on the Passing of Milosz," "A Letter from the Hotel Panorama in Bologna Before Leaving for the Umbrian Jazz Festival," "Eponymous Hard Bop to Horace Silver," and "Art and Death"

Cincinnati Review: "Blues in Blueprint (Alternate Take)," "Eyebrows," and "A Cold Day in March"

Cimarron Review: "'I Begin," "Morning and Night," "A Blues Too Late for Dolphy, 1928-1964," "A Little Pungency, Flood Time," "Two Studies of Two Male Figures," "Montreal Poem," and "Bird Phonetics and Jazz Scat"

Crab Orchard Review: "Granite from Sugar Water" and "St. Vitus' Dance, Teaching Hospital"

diode: "In the Vicinity of Birdfeeders," "Three Odd Ducks on the Atlantic Coast," and "To Cesare Pavese from the Shores of the Mississippi"

The Gettysburg Review: "Cousins of the Heart," "Talkin' to Yourself Blues," "Bluest Thing," "Years after the Hurricane," "Health Care, Taoist Mysticism, and Voodoo," "A Voice from the Spleen," "Plain as Nose on Your Face," and "Repent or Perish"

Pinch: "Thumb in a Blood Orange"

Shenandoah: "Le Printemps de Tucson," "Flesh and Bone," and "Deserts and Oceans"

Straylight: "Wellfleet"

Subtropics: "Mary Sends a Clipping of a Man Who Eats Stones"

I would like to thank Karren Alenier, Jon Anderson, Sandra Beasley, Don Bogen, Robert Olen Butler, Dinah Cox, Bob Cumming, Beto Cumming, Troy DeRego, Deborah Digges, Nancy Eimers, Sascha Feinstein, Becky Hagenston, Edward Hirsch, Richard Howard, Mike Kardos, Dean Karpowicz, Christine Karpowicz, Lisa Lewis, William Matthews, Gary Myers, Bill Olsen, Steve Orlen, Katie Pierce, Rich Raymond, Marty Scott, Jody Stewart, Peter Stitt, David Theis, and David Wojahn.

for Leah Giniusz and Shen Karpowicz

Contents

Part Four

One

"I Begin

logically with chaos, the most natural start. In doing so,
I feel at rest because I may, at first, be chaos myself.
This is the maternal hand." Paul Klee wrote these words.
Beginnings are always this way, spastic tumbleweed,

since there's no "out" to speak of, someone winding a fist
the way people used to mime making a picture, a motion picture,
cranking the camera, trying to keep it focused on someone's face
while shadows undulate like fish across it. Someone will always

disagree with how we might want to proceed, and, besides, inertia
and entropy alter the motion of a venture till it sheds its signature,
like a snake its skin, for all intents and purposes, involuntarily.
So each step is new and generous, even the grizzled father's,

a few incidents ringing like cans fixed to a newlyweds' car
as it pulls out toward the new life, the wisteria blinking.
We start with an idea of where we are, but then events
turn themselves inside out and give us the bum's rush

if they're hard-wired to instinct, if agility is learned in the moment,
if "learned" isn't too crude a way to say this, while integrity,
our raw confidant, taps his foot, waiting on the other end of the line,
foam at the mouth, ringing. We try to audit the annals of regret.

Yes, everyone could've acted better. Our faults eternal as burial vaults
unravel a little malice. In the defunct park, kids pump the sky with a kite.
We fall through a past that really can't be recovered. Who'd want it?
Ignorance and innocence aren't real excuses. We spit them out to speak.

Morning and Night

It will be at least another hour before the sun comes up.
At some point a phone rings—dream scrip snipped and that's it,
a wet straw of breath on your lip. To clean up your act,
use a Kyoto water cannon. You're starting from scratch.
Anything said now would be true on its own laurels.

Paradise is not your milieu—footnote the New York School.
Givens aren't given, they're withheld, and you have to accept that
whether you can reach them, these facts primeval,
catching the red eye express, catching the deadly commute,
whether proximity is relevant, whether action is called for or not.

A grudge is a nest egg you shouldn't nurture,
the center's volatile enough.
You've struck out on your own so many times
impatient clocks keep time with the wick of your heart,
the quick and the dead on the same muddy pavement.

Isn't every consciousness a dark buzzing of neurons?
The porch light pinches the house across the way,
the crepe myrtle a shadow broken away from its lover.
You have to dip your hands in chaos. You don't have to like it.
Dip your axe-handle face. That's the way Howling Wolf,

a.k.a. Chester Burnett, would sing it, as if fresh from a fight.
But someone like Chuck Close stretches the subject's face
into a mural of cross-hatched fields and bays, his own hands
stiffening after the stroke like two exquisite lilies
violating one or more of the aboriginal integrities.

You can't say you've ever taken your time, your own time,
the othering so strong tonight your blood sings with it.
Time passes. Or it doesn't. Say a bird is roused from its nest.
A train horn cuts a distant crossing. An opening door
shoves a yellow wedge into the prickly backside of night.

Two

Cousins of the Heart

Would it have made a difference if I could admit the shame,
as late as it is in terms of modesty, as late as it is in terms of history?
Would it have made a difference to those who pride themselves
on their ability to keep their composure, to those who reason
the way a woodpecker bobs its neck, to those as slick
as ice and cans of motor oil poured over a hairpin curve?
Could it have made a difference to those who wear
the blessed insignia in and out of season, could it have mattered
to the police and the administrators who care for the excellence
of order and money? Could it really have made a difference
once the dam had burst and flooded all the little houses,
once the dead in their coffins bobbed in the current
between the reeds and the slick-edged rocks,
between spring's rebirth and winter's sullenness?
Could it have mattered that I admit the pride
between the gleam of my eye's pupil and its iris,
that I admit the envy and the rage, the wrath bone
like a bomb in the spine? Would it have changed me
to have preferred one past over another,
and could I really say either would have turned out
as I imagined, she with her ease and the other
with her passion, she with her lovely legs, and the other
with the grace of the jaguar, the stealth that feeds nations,
and would I deserve either magnificent life this late
before the redwoods collapse into the sea, before the fires
burn through the properties foundering on cement docks,
before the sun slides into the sea like a casino chip?
Will I ever make peace with the terrier-size bullfrogs
I killed with a stick? Will I ever kiss the green scorpion
I crushed with its rock? I was nine years old in the first case,
twenty-five in the next, still calling my will my desire.
I've gone where the muscles nearly bashed my brains out,
between the rocks and tree roots, down the dank corridors,
between the termite palaces and the tumultuous libraries,
beneath the crisscrossed wires of the trolleys
and the wide open sky. Things have begun to change,
things have begun to feel at home since I've called on the ghost

of Lenny Bruce and slept in the inn named for Catullus
out of respect and out of pleasure, since I crossed the chasm

between the species, even to the feathery tips
of the buds. I can identify with the mourning dove,
a few fingerprints pressed on its wings. I can call
Charles Mingus my petulant brother bear, the cousin of my heart.
I can call the redwing blackbirds my calamitous joy.
They are hinges gone wild, squeaking in the swaying tops
of the pines in my backyard. I can join
these hoarse birds when they fall
like black handkerchiefs to the mud and dry grass.

I could never give up, never learn to do that, no.
I say this not to brag but to lament. Lamenting admits
I won't change in a way I can see. I could hold the vireo in my mouth,
I could make barely audible sounds with the center of my body,
I could open all the windows; all it would take is a hammer with a claw.
All it would take is a chisel; all it would take is the rufous-headed sparrow,
otherwise known as the American with its siblings and in-laws.
The years-old putty and the years-old paint would crack and give.
Eventually the wisteria vines would lift the lintels, encircle the doorjambs.
I could return the shiny lapis, the citrine arrowheads,
the malachite, and the jasper to the damp creases in the earth.
All it would take is a bucket of seawater for the turtle, miles of floss and hair
for the bird nests. I could engage the female cardinal in conversation, a few
primitive peeps at first and, after a few years, a longwinded eventual eloquence
my windpipe would channel, tonsils and muscles alien to the mouth singing.

For Bud Powell: Un Poco Loco

It's part of you, like a finger or deformed toenail,
error offering its solitude, its help.
To travel with error, you walk with nothing else,

your shattered gate a swinging gait—
you don't know which side of the body is which,
one stone or two—one shoe. Desire fills the night,

darkening plantar fascial ache, no time to rest.
You're in it for the long haul, you're in it
for the weakness of desire, its wanting out

and yearning like a bird dog whose existence
is barely recorded before even you tell yourself
that it's illusory, not there, every little thing's

point of view offering its hostile mobility—
life chaos shaded blue. It bears you along like a stick,
street to street, erroneous in your own skin.

The joints will not ache any more than they have to
to get you past death's touch. It's a walk
through Battery Park, desire rotating your ankles,

no untoward incidents occurring along the way, with luck,
something worth experiencing before memory alters it.
You'd like to know the secret—the body you launch

attracting lint and dust, a rosette bruise at the cheek.
After a while, the world room is so crowded
you don't get credit as even a sideman. So very nice,

a consciousness turned that low. One night, you vanished
till they found you teetering between two highways,
bugs lit up by headlights as you swatted through them.

Your sense of being apart from everything as it hovered
assured you some arrogance knew the answers, a few
of these parsed for good beneath your fleet hands.

A Human Throat

I'm making exaltations, I'm making lamentations.
I whistle dirges, uncomfortable with my own excuses.
That's when the angels track me down.
They dance around a dwarf apple tree

filled with beetles already nine-tenths ash and water.
Woodpeckers rehearsing suicide drop from the branches,
black, red and white wrappers changing their minds
at the last second and flying through honeysuckle.

The angels applaud, hooting and hollering.
They construct guitars with wood and wire.
The doves add what they can,
melancholy slipping into release, a musical form.

In my dream I'm shooting a human throat,
a peculiar sort of plasma rifle.
A dog with a black mouth chomps its jaws
on something with a tail, maybe a squirrel.

The angels play acoustic whistle and simple drum,
centuries passing between the first note and the second.
A little leery, I wrestle with the angels.
They can't tell the male from the female body.

It is the touching that thrills them,
hands flexing muscles, the hesitation of ligaments
when the mind sends mixed signals.
I love the way my skin tingles.

I love the smell of my sandals burning.
I look like John Brown, aphasiac grin, beard bristling.
I am ready to pay every last dollar and drop of blood.
I am blowing harmonica past pride and desire.

It is too late to start over. I look like the French painter
far from home, watching his brown-skinned love
lift a clay pot over blue fields of water. Inside it
is the water of satisfaction, inside it is all the time in the world.

In the Vicinity of Birdfeeders

You apologize for being short with the world.
It's not the world's fault.
The world is loquacious with each of us.
The thief's bicycle is nearly camouflaged
in the overgrown towers of mint.
Maybe we *do* take our rewards with us.
Or else we strip away things that no longer hold our interest
and become lighter beings, like gnats or mosquitoes.

Plaster of Paris flakes away from the corners
of the most vigilant projects. Houses of stone
offer more equity over time despite expected vicissitudes,
monsoons and ant mounds. You know the drill.
Does this longevity evaporate like sweat?
We can pray or wage war, pocking someone's stucco.
The angels drank whiskey on your back deck
but never included you in the lively discussion.
Their presence was a comfort,
but they're gone now, with their unwieldy wings.

Granite from Sugar Water

—late 1957

On "Purple Shades," to Johnny Griffin's sax,
Monk plays percussively, stabbing at the keys
as Hardman's trumpet hesitates—the ironic ash
recognizing the loss accomplished—then comes

back in on the beat, and there is nowhere else
to go but on, filling in the gaps, lifting the inarti-
culatenesses, the way the small brown birds lift,
not to abandon something, but to own it, here

on the bark, there, sensed somehow, almost
unperceived, surely not by the antennae nerves
inside the ear, blood blowing across the synapse.
You're the kid with his lips pursed at the mouth

of a bottle sweating cold, leaning back one of those
kinds of chairs a handler jabs at a lion when, peevish,
it strikes out, the way a trombone goes out and back,
out and back, though, in this number, there surely is

no slide to slide, so you have to be vigilant when you
suck the air, distrust raised to art, the way mercury salts
the gills of garfish hovering against a current that ought
to be able to sweep everything out of sight, but doesn't,

can't, those sheaths of cartilage flexing, working hard
to simulate stillness, Monk's missing note, a seventh,
suspending the taste of the imminent, suspending breath,
though the end is on its way sure as everything resists it.

A Blues Too Late for Dolphy, 1928-1964

What makes it through from the past is a lie you make true.
What makes it through from what is whole and lost to you
is the image of a woman's back, its curve, the horizon line—
the way back. What makes it through is your horn's lisp

hissed for a demo-tape, *whee, twheee*. Did you, do you
sound like that, your heart retuned in the time between?
Are you lost too? What makes it through from yesterday
is the old melody unstrung from the vertebrae's airy harp

and played back on itself, notes bent as far as they might,
most of these, sharp, shaded lavish blue and irretrievable.
West coast kid, you wet the reed with your tongue and lips,
blew tweets for the finch nattering in your mother's thicket.

Now shadowtime filters dust down the ridge of your nose,
your face in profile as on a coin, your goatee like Ramses'
jutting out, Adam's apple tunneling the earth of your throat.
The stand-up is thumping at what is breakneck. A rim shot.

And what's this, the keyboard rushing like a brown current
yawning grief it's hauled too long. Half note before the beat—
slide rule's slip—you know you'll not recover who you are.
And the future cries uncle down the sleeve with magic's hare.

We story this so everything and nothing hurts, eardrum's snare
vibrating skin. Mingus, walking the bass, feathers the sounds
while muscles kiss back reliable ache. Survival tactics in B flat.
The pianist plays an atoll of notes, out and back, stick at the rim.

Slowly the regulars clap, chins in motion for all that, the bass,
extra-amp'd, thumping fast. You push tempo against time's lapse—
limit lashed—as if what hasn't happened yet were already past.
Shouldn't you be giddy, old ghost, blood at your neck like sap?

Blues in Blueprint (Alternate Take)

Like a launch above its inboard motor, like a red-tailed hawk
dropping through mist, like distant smoke, he lets himself drift.
He'll have to take more than the usual paths to find surprise
this late in the century, that is, if he doesn't wizen into ire,

suck it behind his teeth and swallow it, to start his day.
Would he warn his Jackself to *leave comfort root-room*,
the tendrils taking over, someone in the back of the theater
clapping his hands, the projector whirring white on white,

time's augur confessing wider flow? The fields of childhood
are what he unsigns his name to, the uneasiness of pictures
half-emerging from his past, whatever epithet will jump start
the nervous system and tremble the fingers with it, with some

sort of integrity. A troubling integity is probably permitted
in circumstances in which the trellises of dented hubcaps
and strangled saxes cry out with a fierce forgetfulness,
a tailor's torso waiting to unleash a sample thrashing,

the way, one night, snow banking its murderous sublimities,
he ran the keys, the speed turning the tempo inside out,
to protect him from himself, like handcuffs hung on a nail,
as if some saint's slipped disc had slipped its reliquary,

the sight of which burnt his retina almost opalescent.
Each day he has to do this, as if memory has to be re-cued
in the early hours before the whitetail slip past the birch
to thicker woods. The hiss of traffic from the highway

is a sound he barely dares acknowledge, cars speeding past
as the sunlight fades behind the pines and every elsewhere
ceases palpably to exist—an imploding black ever-present inch.
Each note starts out to kick something off, but then it doesn't.

It calls those who'll do what it tells them to, who'll play each lick
the way each lick would want itself played, eavesdropping the blood.
Inspiration might arrive in the guise of a tire shot across a field
or a lightning strike dividing a scrub oak with a new music

that darkens to ash like beard trimmings inking a puttied sink.
His composition must swing in some succinct way. Sometimes,
when he gets back to it, it's flown the coop, some little bird sound
from the shadows beneath trees, the crackle of twigs just before

the horns would blow the heavens in. On the roof next door,
a man calls down to men spreading plans on the hood of a car.
In an hour, the shadows across the yard have literally shifted,
the new shapes cutting light, its fabric. It's not catastrophic,

but how can a venture not cut naming loose if he enters it,
the name being the stingiest part of the going, his trying
not to ruin other people's enjoyment of the act, even if the act,
if up to them, ain't up to it, his wanting it to be otherwise.

He wears loose-fitting clothes, every hope a hand-me-down,
shine-worn and threadbare, not that there's anything wrong
with a stiff curve of starch getting the shit kicked out of it.
As he waters the Russian sage—half of which is thriving,

tiny blowtorch blue buds—a toad jumps, a soap bubble pricked,
like a self-consciousness so intensely pure all is gone for good.
Not much realty, these anxious hours he keeps people's bodies
barely in sight, through a scrim of blue-tinted pine. One day,

four strays thrash a cat in the air, killing it—its tongue lolled.
It takes years of listening, but he thinks he knows the sound
of accident as it happens. He lets the world sound through him,
even if it hems and haws, a thing barely able to cut a word loose.

Talkin' to Yourself Blues

Those by the sliding door look like pharaohs, lapis-painted eyes.
They hip sway, drinks in hand, memorializing time's happiness.

Another word on this would just be story. That you must forget
is not amputation or even benevolent self-improvement. At times

you're lucky what's past remains whole and at a distance, memory
an obsessive house cleaner, a faint stench in its rag. Days gone by

cut acrid timbre. What it comes down to is you doubt God's kiss,
you doubt your doubt's good naturedness. Memory conjures events

from a past, part and parcel of how you step from the past and haven't
with each new step. What then, declare the rest a mess, less legitimate

because it's thick with indeterminateness? Can you close your eyes
till unconsciousnesss—pure neutrality—births itself? Is that God too?

Here's one for a pitch so high even the barmaid's dogs sleep through it.
Here's one for the close quarters. Riding the sonic edge of pleasure out,

Shaw flexes his fingers, fidgeting the valves of his trumpet, spraying spit,
bass thumbing the heart's slackening beat. The drummer flicks the rim,

but the band doesn't speed up, not right away, that is. J.J. shifts his slide,
all halftime bluster euthanized. Cowlicked pianist lips hiccups and growls

to stand for the sleazy side of things, the blood flush, the itch, how it feels
when—ignored—you go on speaking, embarrassed blather slipping to elision.

Blues on the Passing of Milosz

Dragonfly pinched in the beak, a female swallow lights on a line,
its scissors-tail vexed and empty, slick as the sky seen through it.

If you say the fig leaves are heart-shaped, that's not right.
Your parents die. That's exact. You'll die when the time comes.

And what of that? Those sweet figs that impersonate genitals—
you know the ones, swathed in fluted paper—they never last.

While you're asleep, the racoons must feast, sagging the branches
like feted Greeks, dark-eyed sailors bathed in refracted moonlight.

Or else you aren't sleeping, out walking the deep curve of ditches—
aloneness like spit in a mouthpiece, blue pines swaying the dark.

You clap your hands after the weak beat, a hesitating dot duration,
whipping the mind's slick dithering, broom driving something off.

A boy, grown up and pissed, you feel God stuck beneath your ribs,
swallowed by the heart—what jolts the nerve before music starts.

A Letter from the Hotel Panorama in Bologna
Before Leaving for the Umbrian Jazz Festival in Orvieto

—for William Matthews

Bill, I'm here again and, of course, down the corso
two towers tilt toward each other, like old lovers
a little drunk, going home. In a restaurant, I savor
a little glass of grappa next to an attractive couple.

The woman leans, curls a tortellini on her tongue
and hums, no, moans a quiet song, not exactly that,
but a sound I might hope for her after they climb
five flights to their room and have sex, slide off

laughing to the floor. No one knows who they are
if they die or do not return home: the thought I had
outside the station, how I might, by some abandon,
buy a jacket, collar up, with a scarf to mask my lips,

and then slip, unnoticed, down one *bin* or another
into another not necessarily beautiful life. Of course,
I've already slid, amateur voyeur pitching a woman
as some high-wire acrobat above the circus. What

could I do with my old-fashioned hook and ladder
when the whole city is on fire? I lie in bed, the décor
a pale blue sky with puffs of cloud. Whenever I want,
I can take the cage lift to the café tables on the street.

But there's all day to unfurl the body from its envelope,
the train to the City Built on Tufa doesn't leave till five.
Once there, I'll take the funicular to the Pozzo Etrusco.
After dinner, the owners invite each one of their diners,

in turn, down a circular stairwell to the base of the cistern.
Space is a little tight, but there is no roar of time, no vertigo
as you stand there with yourself. Minutes later, you're back
to order dessert or another drink. I recommend the moscato.

Eponymous Hard Bop to Horace Silver

You dub songs "Silverware," "Horoscope," "Quicksilver,"
and even "Knowledge Box," bashed planks spilling silver,
the hard bop tempo hellbent to nowhere if it isn't the end
where warehouses stick up like teeth around the switches.

At the stroke of an elbow, cars uncouple to piles of salt,
steam in plumes rising from the scent of diesel and wire.
Surely this conduit hive inspires—three-deckers in rows
masting soot-stained brick with bedsheets and flannels,

with de-elasticized boxers bored with the wind's fingers,
the smell of bleach scenting the iron rust of fire escapes
where hands drum whatever gives back the most sound
for the least motion, a form of hope too tough for speech.

Your flat-fingered puncturing breaks through, note for note,
a pulse the blood believes when the envious gods sleaze in
and make it hard, your saxman slumped off the commode,
top of his head tipped to the wall, knuckles pressed in gum.

The bartender's boy ferries small dirty white cups of coffee,
the man's trousers a black froth at his ankles. *Use the lady's,*
for Christsake. Slow now, take it easy. Man, I said... ok,
catch him under the arms, that's it. Good. Come on, pal.

An hour late, eyes slit, he's crossing the spotlight, hand out
darkening the beam. The band hesitates, stiff and out of sync,
but, breaking through rage to refigure it, you lift the tempo.
Lee lofts the trumpet, piping spit into light, half-valving it.

Then you curve your shoulder over the keys, cowlick tossing
a Cape Verdean groove, muscles aching the back of your hand.
You treat the piano as the percussive box it is, explosive turns
forcing the sax to swerve corrosive, fricative, slightly hoarse.

Blue neon shapes slice soundwaves out of memory's earshot,
the sweet lies, fear and delight, staving off hounding loneliness.
The stand-up plays a counter beat, then falls in line, the sticks
flying from hi-hat to ride cymbal, dragging the backbeat home.

Three

A Mouth

A sack of marbles, worthless coins, say what you will.
A mausoleum of teeth, stale saliva.
What's behind the lips is a geyser.
Count from ten to one hundred.
Patience is impossible, a device to elongate eternity.
What's wrong with that? If the past comes back
we won't recognize it so when it disowns us,
everything will be mutual, evanescent, and when,
like a starlet, it blow us kisses, there won't be any hard feelings.

Thumb in a Blood Orange

Will my manservant take the battle axe from a chain-mail fist
that, when I open it, is a wicket of precise widgets?
Will he sheathe the broadsword after he cleans it,
blood returning to the earth so next spring's impatiens
blossoms blood red over the rocks, a red water?
My lance is shattered at the hilt. Funny how the tales
innumerate the arms. The Luger, the handgrenade,
the machine gun, the sock knife. All I can do now
is fall to my knees. All I can do now is lift the acidic skin
from the tomato with my teeth. My iridescent parakeet
loops the blades of the ceiling fan, unscathed dragon budgie.
I pick rue in the garden, the bitter white tips of basil.
There is room for their inanities, there is room for mine.

When the drummer tosses his cymbal to chase Parker from the stage,
cruelty saves jazz from the dance floor. Bird begins woodshedding
how his sax might kill, splitting the notes like no one before him.
He packs so much into a solo because poor kids know there's no time
for patience or forgiveness. Clifford Brown doesn't hustle his friends
the way Parker has to. Neither of these men lives very long,
so living into my fifties, I'm culpable of wanting my breath
to count for something, guilty of wanting some distinction.
That's why I love the blood oranges in the market at Montmartre.
That's why I love the circular breathing of the saxophonist
I heard on the side of the Campo one night in Siena.
That's why I disembowel avocadoes, the television blaring,
the old stereo blaring, flecks of green shaving cream on my chin.

I'm testing how many different ways I can cut time, hear it back
across the depths of the inner ear. I'm trying to refuse
the separation between the world and my body. When I was born,
the umbilical cord strangled me garrulous. If I waste the words the right way
they're not wasted, they are part of the sonic fog that is me and isn't.
That's why identity is a ruse and destiny is a child's invention.
In the shithouses, Lenny Bruce aims his words at comfort and power.
It isn't the words so much as the motions they engender.

The horn players are the only ones who get Lenny's jokes
when he bombs at the Blue Haven in Jackson Heights.
The way the woodpecker freefalls from grub to spider
and from sunflower to worm, the wind's edge
is a part of my cry dipping through the thin sheath
of scum over a furrow. It's improvisation's unsteady stint.
My neighbor's oak suspends spoons and forks by wires,
a rusted not-so stainless song. Sometimes their sulking
swings in an unheard register. The woodpecker
swivels its head, and I mention this because every nuance,
whether it's picked up on or not, is in on it,
this gambit of mine, a blade nick on Gawain's neck,
the woodpecker's red nape line, Lenny's string of curses
like the spittle of life itself. Dear lord, it's a colorful language.

I get a little crazy, jump in the car and drive the country roads.
I pull over at a spot where a tree root erupts
because this might be the place to abandon infinity for good.
I love the weeds for their brokenness and their prayer.
I love their hirsute exhalations in a hurry to do nothing at all.
Three bison kick up clods with hooves trodding what must,
by local standards, pass for a park. A child cups a palm of dry feed.
The bison's cumbersome bodies barely move,
spittle swerving their chins and beards.
I must say that their droppings are lavish. Is that the right word?
If I pretend to behave, will a second woodpecker alight on the bison,
warble *chucklehead, chucklehead*, congenial as a cheerleader at tryouts?
If I take the kid by the hand when the bison move like ships in harbor
will I feel fatherly or worse, concerned with the safe and long life?
It's growing colder, the tops of the trees are swaying.
I could say it's grown darker, the cold does that, makes a person
imagine gradual darkening. The field recedes when the sun backs off,
I can feel it, my larger blood backing off my smaller.

Eyebrows

Do these epaulettes designate rank
in some humiliated army?

Or are they the wings of a distant hawk,
the punctuation marks

above Apollo's empty eyes? One man
licks his pinkie and strokes his eyebrows.

A second man touches them with his fingertips.

Bluest Thing

Two or three baby-fingernail sharp blue buds
above bark dust shine so much bluer than the saint

traced in black on the stained glass,
the blue arrows winging home, his trunk a stolid tree.

Nothing's worth dying, Yang Chu writes,
it's the same whether you bury or leave me in the open,

throw me in a ditch, wrapped in grass,
or lay me in a stone coffin, dressed in a dragon-blazoned jacket.

At a Quaker meeting house, seventeen, standing since noon
in moratorium, praying the jets would run out of bombs,

I watched a jay trapped somehow, redundantly flexing its wings
above bare rafters, the bluest thing in its urgency.

Mary Sends a Clipping of a Man Who Eats Stones

Now is the winter to lift a shaky voice, *now* is nothing
you can keep, proceedings you recuse yourself from,
a palmed Ace toward the floor. *Now* continues to move,
an Adam's apple lifting just as the player piano unrolls
"Begin the Beguine," then "Take Me Out to the Ballgame."

Will it let you get back to your riffs, a riot of disinclination
inspired by inches of rain? You tote empty wire cages
into a room, trying not to implode into a coward's version
of what struggles in your throat, the American goldfinch,
an air as airy as that, blessing or no. The tongue untwists

like a wisp of steam. Do you have to perfect being alone?
Is that God, too? You want to rearrange the compedium
of integral facts but sink in a roadside ditch. Flower books
agree swampwort thrives on neglect. If fatigue takes you,
should you resist? As you leg it over the hill, the sun sets.

Been compromised. Collective Promise, as airy as this,
a truck rolls by, its back latticed with feathers. Adepts say
Heft a stone for your pillow, and peace fills your limbs.
All you can picture is the moon over the sea, a feral scrawl.
You'll have to start from scratch, you'll have to start with

the airy cyphers, whatever emptiness might be depicted as,
what chickens peck at: part refuse, part roughage, part rain,
demolition and groundbreaking, a spade stepped into clay.
To give flesh to dream, is there room for all these shames?
There's the photo of an Afghani who swears he eats stones,

and, given the lack of evidence to the contrary, who's to say,
he's not the genius the world will soon have to reckon with?
The twilight is a reckless taking of breath, an expressiveness
the heart needs, nicking softly the notions of poise and tact
so you can keep a fitful sleep, the sound of a wave breaking

as though inside you was the patience to twist a feather duster
through all the little exotic baubles, the exploding souvenirs,
so as not to topple what is comfortable with simply residing.
There's so much room ghosts slip soundlessly from sleeves
no one calls *his*. Sleep as fast as you can—a musician's joke.
To lie across time, the mind shut-off, not even time working....

Talk About Crazy

This is the year the dead come back
in blazing headdresses.
J. Edgar sports a spoiled diaper.
Faubus blows smoke off his index finger.
LBJ flaps his ears for the camera.
This is the year the shock jocks
take a vow of silence.
This is the year they learn a gag reflex.
This is the year they slip off the cowls
to reveal their delicate pates.
This is the year I take them
on a wild goose chase.
They watch me touch the pullets
swaying on gallows strings.
They watch me touch pig brains
with the tip of my pinkie.
Of course, I'm doing this for pleasure.
Of course, I confess a little contempt.
Joe McCarthy plays with his ear
while he's speaking into the microphone.
Jolting Joe touches Marilyn's elbow.
This is the year I cease counting teeth.
All indices insist this is the year of abundance.
This is the year my feet begin moving.
I vault two stairs at a time in ashen light.
The citrine points predict the end of longing.
The lapis lazuli laps up the oceans of sorrow.
This is the year of elation, the lungs lifting.
I've trashed my uncomfortable shoes.
I've turned in my scowl. Enough broken mirrors.
I've turned in all my coupons, confetti, confetti.
I slip and spike my tailbone, each step separate,
one forward, one back, not exactly folk dancing.

I won't wait for the remembering to start.
I won't wait for the ceremonies to begin.
I'm swimming in the midst of unhurried otters.

The slicked-back fur and small black claws
steer me through cathedrals of algae.
I'm not against they're drawing me
over underwater cameras. I'm not against
anything anymore. Once I reach the beach,
I will lie on my back and breathe.
Then I will pull my left knee to my chest,
fingers clasping inflexible muscle cord and fat.
I'm starting over, starting with the number zero.
So much for citations and manifestoes,
so much for triumph and satisfaction.
I've turned in my trimmed syllables.
This is the year of bountiful commodities.
I strike a match to the marsh punk and reeds.
It's about time cars coast the new causeway
and watch me dance among tunnels of smoke.
Maybe I should shave my head and grow a beard.
I could get used to baggy trousers tied with rope.
I could trap the lizards and cook them on sticks,
eventually become inconspicuous, even to the trees.

Ted Kennedy kisses Mary Jo's terse lips.
My buzzing mind still bends me at the knees,
checks my gait, tick, tock, and reaches up
to pluck fruit just out of reach, peach or plum.
Maybe as I reach up to a bulb on a string
and the filament clicks and blinks out,
I remember the doctor taking my immobilized
index finger and saying "This is the light bulb"
and tapping my C-6, "But this is the switch."
I couldn't make a fist for months.
Call it fear or deliberation or animal instinct—
it doesn't care what it's called. Before this,
I wouldn't have given you a cent for talismans.
Now I have so many, my place looks like a crypt:
a jade horse for pageantry, a rabbit for luck,
a boat carved from lapis for passage
to the underworld, even a mummified gazelle
I cut from a *National Geographic*.
I'm trying not to feel the bird inside my ribs.

I'm going over the irretrievable years.
Lazarus is mumbling *not this again*.
I can't taste the lips of those who've stayed behind.
I don't blame my passage on the wind or the waters.
Suddenly the skies recede like bamboo fans.
There will be no need for excitement or music.
There will be no thirst, no ants on the march.
Thelonious Monk will cease brooding, the left hand
across the right to hobble every last key.
Once I surprised the catcher's mask and guitar picks
scattered on the chest guard at the bottom
of my parents' closet, my mother's hat
that looks like a delicate bird nest singed in hell.
But I can't put my finger on any of these things now.

Talk about crazy, I blew a chance to hear Mingus
in sweltering Greenwich Village, 1979.
The cabbie deposited us at the best club in town,
since we'd asked for it. I hadn't learned patience.
I still haven't. We did something else. We were young.
I can't say what I was doing when Mingus lifted
like a spoonbill looking like a roseate spit off the sun.
I've memorized every fantasia he ever dreamt
before his nerves finally betrayed him the same year.
I can't say which is my favorite. My favorite
is "Fables of Faubus" or "The Haitian Fight Song."
"Prayer for Passive Resistance" knocks me out.
This is the year I'll kiss my mother's wedding ring
for the luck of the Irish, the crazy Irish.
What will a year of forgiveness do for my body?
I give you my tired lips, my limp arms.
Maybe scarcity will cease to hold sway.
This is the year I fold my shirts, flip the sleeves
across the buttons, and stack them in drawers,
the threadbare corduroys and the bold Hawaiians.
So what if I speak in falsetto to the cat?
So what if the synapses between my nerves burn hot?
Can I cease planning the next assignation?
Do I empty the roof of my mouth?
Do the backs of my eyes turn white?

I'm ready for love to take over my body.
I will have to rewire my nerves, teach my hands
to swoop and dive like sparrows.
I will practice silence on the fig tree and rotted fence.
The spider lilies take root where they can. One step,
and a bird crashes from brush, an affronted queen.
It took me years to admit the nuptials of pride and desire.
And once I did, what then, what next?
I will have to wait and see about beauty and grace.
I will have to wait and see about the body's resilience.
The sunflowers drop their heads, old mannequins
with broken necks. The blackberries abscess all at once,
as if each one has to prove its absentmindedness.
I can repeat the furtive gesture of fingertips to tongue,
fingertips to tongue like a squirrel or chipmunk.
I'm not boasting, I'm barely breathing, one lung
kindling, one lung accelerant, the kiss of incandescence.

Years after the Hurricane

If I cross my shadow, undo my life
like a stick of gum its wrapper,
if I abide near the sea,
at least for a while, let no one
take offense or action against a man
eating dove eggs from a statue's lap.
Will I forgive the receding I can't recall?
I watch a welder on his scaffold
sway on the side of a gray tanker.
Sparks from a torch flick off his visor
and rasp like bees on the dock.
I grimace a pill down, no water.
I see a woman reading on a bench.
I try to pass without distracting.
But I wonder if a luxurious wave
of seaweed were to plunge from the top
of her scalp, would I whisper in her ear,
and would she remember what I say
years later as her saddest memory?
I defy the last human ingenuity.
If I shave my head, wear a cap in sun
and a toboggan against the cold,
maybe I can own up to human performance
and confess how honesty is twisted with art
inside our sweet obsession with privacy.
No matter how many dance the street
in feathered headdresses, the years of want
will come. No matter the number of destitute,
the years of fat will follow the angry times.
If my desires assume time's rounded shape,
if they assume its ancient erasure,
maybe I can forgive what I can't recall.
My velocities make the wind hungry.
Should I sign the confession in triplicate,
bear down on the pencil so my signature
will be legible on the flimsy carbons?

At Palm Court Café, the old virtuoso
plays trumpet without fanfare, two mics
picking up the giddy clarinet. Leah
orders a drink she hears the waitress
call out to the barmaid who tells us
the mix for a sazerac must be exact
and she is one of the best in town
for getting that right mix of whiskey,
simple syrup, glass coated with Pernod.
Next day I'm drinking tea in a shop.
Sea stink permeates the woodwork.
The goth clerk talks about an herb
that flushes toxins from the heart.
I will stay for the quiet and the artifacts,
the voodoo dolls and a thousand Buddhas.
I've arranged my aching tailbone
between the sky and the porous wall.
I hear the sound of my salty blood.
Suddenly I'm driving an apple orchard at twilight.
We look for deer, pop-outs she calls them,
a few already craning their necks, accomplices
tearing with their teeth to pull down the stars.

A Little Pungency, Flood Time

I start in the basement, palms pressed to the wall
where the earth sweats through. I smooth my pages.
I am reading the fabliaux for my Irish aunts
for there are thousands, I am reading the Veda

for Lenny Bruce and his repertoire's sweet mouth,
for Caliban picking white grubs from tree roots,
for John Doyle who smashed his fist against my lips
where there are thousands of capillaries feathering red.

I am dissecting my lips because the hatred is there,
I am pushing my palms down on the long thighs
as if measuring distance to start a tunnel
that can't possibly reach beyond the enclosure,

even if I taste the dirt in my nose. My hair is curling.
I am bringing back the shit flocked over the playroom
from the chickens and cocks I raised as a boy,
the black claws for style, the red wattle for survival.

Out in the yard, I remember ten strides to each one of mine.
Did I take that hunger for love, matted feathers bowed low?
I am paying attention to the mudflats, the tubers
turning over on invisible fins. I am collecting pinecones.

The sharp tips train my hand to an inhuman delicacy.
If I can drain the soil so the roots won't sit in glut,
I can teach a few derricks of feathery dill to flourish.
I require a little pungency in my life, I think I have to risk it.

I'm driving past the bait shops. If I can pluck a pillow
from the flood waters, from snakes and slugs in their glory,
all will seem well for a while and the blood will quiet.
The lizard egg I will save for the silence and its questions.

If I can pity the armadillo's armor, the cicada's hull,
If I can dry out the chest protector and catcher's mask,
maybe the words will wash away with the dissatisfaction.
There will be a little pungency at the tip of my tongue.

If I can salvage a big-eyed parrot, one ancient astrolabe,
if I can blow humility through the bones of my sinuses,
maybe I can assume the diminutive role I was meant for,
if I can burn off all the last of my impurities.

I am auditing the silence, I am chewing my wormy lips,
signatures sighing in the flames. I hack pride with a pickaxe,
I hack desire in the process. It feels strange to touch the world.
It feels strange to own up to meanness and ancient sorrow.

Health Care, Taoist Mysticism, and Voodoo

An earache shoots through my skull
like heat lightning—intermittent—O,
worthy bone cap, please grant me lull
if not cease. My foot turns on the big toe,

bone anchor dragging dirt. Does the brain
express the excruciating ache and repeat it
beneath all the weight gravity forces back
down upon my ugly but serviceable foot?

My body is looking for a loyalty oath
so the voodoo priest plants a green bottle
in the earth. After a while, a whole phalanx
marches the yard while the evil spirits

haunt the periphery, trying to materialize.
Sun glints off the bottles like battlements.
At least it's not the pullet's pimpled flesh.
Some men and women get life and death

at the times they wish, and some live and die
when it's not time to live and die. Lieh-tzu,
your words rise at the rift. Chickens peck
at the dirt one day, circle it headless the next.

A cat crosses the grass beneath the spirit house
hung from crepe myrtle. Ghosts love agile limbs.
A single spiderwort takes root where it can—
indigo eye, benevolent Cyclops, intensely shy.

Four

A Voice from the Spleen

What if the negotiations end in apples or oranges,
oranges or apples, and the old way of cutting a crisp feather
across the canvas is a vast depth of time that up till now
you thought you were supposed to dedicate yourself to?
The words form on your lips like platform divers,
wanting to touch bottom, no splash. The bloody fingerprint
has degraded too much to provide a match to your identity,
thumb and fingertips rolled in ink. These records are on file,
but a clerical error has released you to roam at large,
largely harmless and shocking to yourself. What if your spleen
like a ferris wheel car rocks with night wind, unoccupied—
or like sticks of TNT with a detonating wire that's come loose—
do you feel uncommitted to the very next breath you take?
What if there's no song for this? What if the acerbic shrill
of a gilt kazoo is the museum of music you were meant to lisp?
What if Camus was right about the butterfly wing burnt to ash
in a forest fire, a memory so lost it sings with an inhuman voice?

A Cold Day in March

The French philosopher daydreams about the great American outdoors. Yes, Albert Camus, the French existentialist philosopher, tugs the worm through the hook and then lowers it a few feet into the water. The fish rise. A few fish get some ease to eat. A few gargle grit. Above his head a few hundred miles, wisps of clouds begin to gossip in a dialect that might be a cross between Paper Clip and Old Crustacean. Clouds like whips. The leaves blow. On one side, they are bright, on the other, a hazy dun color. The vireos eat bits of bread from the Frenchman's hand. He's more Saint Francis of Assisi than Ernesto Hemingway. He chuckles. Then it is late, he's thinking, but for what he can't say.

Now the birds are high in the apology trees. Apology trees look like discarded tissues, if one is far enough away to see them as a French philosopher would see them, thoughts like saturated air wanting to snow.

Plain as the Nose on Your Face

About one of these, Gogol had plenty to say,
plain as a blank piece of paper.

Plain as sand, biscuit, wafer,
like a butte over arid plains.

If a man is practiced in self-defense,
he may drive the nose like a spike

into his assailant's brain,
the heel of the hand in an upward thrust.

But everyone is calm tonight,
everyone is happy with the arrangements.

A man blows a trumpet sputter
into a checkered handkerchief.

A few hairs scatter. Ah, the early lilacs.

Le Printemps de Tucson

Like Harpo Marx, R. can grin at a girl's lapel pin. Like Groucho, he can kill a fly with the tip of a whip.

Few people want to live their lives as an experiment the way R. does, maybe by choice or the convenient appearance of choice, moustache quavering or beatific dumb moon.

It's a spring night, Gate's Pass. Wrens sweep the ancient cacti. An actual roadrunner coos a soliloquy, six low notes. It is barely illuminated. It throbs direction, but no particular one, an abstract pleasure.

Flesh and Bone

It's hard to be sure. A man grapples with his own body. Or he grapples with a lover's body, the wing of an elbow caught like a gull in a wave's suction till it surrenders what looks like a dollop of black blood spun in centrifuge.

A circle circumscribes their love, making the figures look like a duffel bag and maybe a few pairs of socks tossed around a commercial dryer at a Laundromat. It's probably late in the evening, some large city. Everyone else is sleeping. Or every other human body is experiencing a similar turbulence, and all will be well in a little while. This is one panel of Bacon's "Three Studies of Figures on Beds."

In Giacometti's "City Square" five thin figures cross in various directions a slightly warped plane of black stone. They are beehive threads that never intersect.

R. looks out the window across the winter garden. The mint twisted with hoarfrost and mould chokes a stick to look like an old man with a dowager's hump. It's not as if R. might hold off the freezing temperatures or contrive a body more consummate with shame.

He wants to write a poem as still as a sleeping cat. One of the earliest cats in history slept while Buddha was dying. There is no reason to mourn. No one should blame the grace of a cat curled into an imperfect circle or, for the matter, a cat scaling a fire escape as effortlessly as a trapeze artist.

There are so many beautiful bones in the Museum of Natural History. The stingray's skeleton looks like a chain mail set of wings.

Over millennia, one of the flounder's eyes migrates so that it rests cockeyed next to the other, not on either side of the head as in most fish. The dorsal bone swerves behind the eye sockets, these asymmetrical settings for black opals.

Off the coast of Maine, R. sees a group of flounder through green silt and sea. It doesn't seem like memory, this image: five or six of them on a sandbar a few feet below the surface, the boat barely moving.

Art and Death

1. Body Works, Roma

Georgio DeChirico raised an earth cloud
above parapets with male nudes posed
like preening eagles so I'm not repulsed
as much as unnerved by the dead bodies

arrogant as mannequins, nerves like plied
fiber optic tines. Half in earnest, I sign up
to become one of the exhibit's specimens.
As garden homunculi, we all stoop and fly,

the Wright Brothers of memento mori
pretending we'll live forever. What else
might hope remember? One of the bodies
cradles a separate head the way a child

carries an oversized book to show and tell.
A third flies a horse on wires above lights
till everything begins to recede, or worse,
loom up and say everyone is unwelcome

in this room, eavesdropping on the elements.
How did Actaeon become meat for his dogs?
Didn't they recognize his scent? Or perhaps
he grew so sorely other he set upon himself.

*2. Francesco Signorelli's "The Allegory of the Immaculate
Conception," Cortona; Luca Signorelli's frescoes in the Duomo,
Chapel of San Brizio, Orvieto*

The museum in Cortona had a painting lit so dimly
I could barely see it, worse now with memory's eye,
that cataract that fits both definitions of the word.
Most likely, there are more than two meanings for it,

but you know which two I mean, the opaque swerve
across the eye and the tears that plummet like a river
suddenly—we can't say why our desires complicate.
He paints God the Father and Mary larger than life.

But I want to note the narrow base of this colossus
where the figure of Adam lifts a hand to warn Eve,
the way the altar boys swing the censer over the hip
on holy days, the limited human scale in the humble

odor of smoke. I'll take experience over reverence,
any chance at counterbeat. Is that why I had to scoff
at your fear of the open Etruscan graves on the hillside
because the space grew agape and seemed to welcome

any ole fool, stone cut wide, a patch of green grass
that to stand on didn't feel menacing so bright the air
was when we climbed down from the city? When I
play Coltrane's "Giant Steps" I think of that morning,

my lungs filling with air. I play it, my lungs emptying.
Some wind like this must have crossed Luca Signorelli's
heart while he hung from a scaffold to work the frescoes
above the tufa. He painted himself into the world's end

and into the light that exudes from the resurrected nudes
who can't restrain their limbs on the opposite chapel wall.
The bodies push up from the surface, their elbows flexing—
the new bodies stand straight, the skin for once triumphant.

3. *The New Orleans Strutters, Territory Band Ghosts*

Back when, we'd improvise to trick ofays,
but, nowadays, they love the ordinariness
so much we brandish our chops, and none
show up to find out what laws we broke.

So far we've survived, not taking root.
The honeysuckle vines hook our sleeves
whenever we slow down enough to sit.
Do we look like we were born last night,

a feral mother pinching us in her teeth?
We practice going without, and, damn,
we're pretty good at it. We use the wind
and the lack of it, croak the merit of birds

and tap out a raucous dirge in the trees,
sleeping as fast as we can, switching time
so deftly we humiliate the local hot-shots.
In the car, momentum drums out miles,

backache's pulse cutting motion's drone.
Death is continuous, not the last erasure
blurring our names and dates like chalk.
We swing tall cadet caps over the bells

so the brass will mute the joy loss takes
for a ride above the empty ballroom dark,
a screech on sax, the slide inching back,
just so silence can't have the final word.

Three Odd Ducks on the Atlantic Coast

I'm wearing a beryl stone with the image of a hoopoe.
I'm wearing it on a leather loop around my neck.
I can feel it stick to my chest so I free it with fingers,
an adjustment. I click the hairline break in my ankle
that never quite healed after I climbed the back wall
playing racquetball like some stupid Superman.
I click it because I can and there is some pleasure
in flaunting most versions of adversity. I click my own
wretched survival, using my tongue, using my fingers.
With a sprig in its beak, this crazed Old World woodpecker
lets me talk with the dead, two in particular who died
under suspicious circumstance. We walk past the cliffs,
past the skyscrapers, past the dank estuaries and isles.
In a sweatshirt hood, Pasolini looks like a squire,
his mouth and nose a poor stray's muzzle.
Sand sifting where he steps, he says he can't recall
his assailants' faces—his own blood everywhere
as one of the men turns and howls at the sea,
lifting his hands to the night sky. One of their faces
was exultant, he says, like the crucified saint's.
Pasolini says men in Italy just break into song
right on the street, but not the women, the young ones,
thin and hurrying. Frank O'Hara says his death was awful,
but he clams up, mum as Lazarus, the friend for whom
Jesus wept, imagine that, to have a friend weep like that.
Frank O'Hara would rather talk about the new paintings
his own friends are working on, Larry Rivers,
Joan Mitchell. Grace Hartigan, Michael Goldberg.
I don't recognize all the names, maybe they're artists,
maybe they're longshoremen or hermaphrodites,
Frank loves so many different forms of beauty,
the lovely man. There's sand in his hair, he's talking
with his hands the way I do, the way we all do,
like birds' wings a bit flustered at a feeder,
fixated on seeds. We're all talking at once when,
all of a sudden, I don't know what's got into me,
I launch into the air, coming down on the muck

from an old jellyfish, purple or white, it's hard to tell
it's so dark—sorry, Jolly Roger, sorry, Treasure Island,
sorry, Peg Leg Pete. I step on a small rusted nail,
maybe part of an old ship or part of a boathouse
blown off in a storm. It's all right, what's a little blood,
what's a little rust, it's wonderful, isn't it: oxidation,
I mean, my heels hard as doorknobs from walking?
Frank starts singing "Last Night I Got Loaded"
with a British, with a Mexican, with a lithe swagger.
I'm balancing on a seawall, spoofing in falsetto
"Brandy, you're a fine girl," a plaintive bubblegum love,
O the blind fifties, its grisly head still above water.
I sing Pier Paolo Pasolini, and he says, "Get it right,
you poor Irish Yankee"—all his wonderful Italian vowels
in my mouth: Pier Paolo Pasolini, Pier Paolo Pasolini!
3 P's, I'm giggling, and he loves my coinage, the thought
of it: perseverance, pleasure, peace. We recite it black
as the night is black because the sea swallows our voices
and adds its own. We're like gulls stopping and starting,
crossing private rights of way as well as public beaches,
the rocks and dirt on one side, the waves on the other.
We heave stones and shells into the waves, we heave
our own clumsy bodies. The water is cold and the wind
makes us shiver. My sleeves droop like the angel's wings
on the side of the Duomo in Milan, my pant-legs stick.
3 P's is sweeping back his hair. He's a handsome demon
and a frustrated gargoyle, either and both. The sun is just
starting to make the night albescent—I love that word— its
cradle cap still beneath the horizon—the dark, as they say, lifting.

Two Studies of Two Male Figures

(San Diego)

When I think of you, it's outside—the lights from chinks
terraced erratically down the shale cliffs.
The first happiness rises from the night sea like a fog.
The whole shore is music sloshing waves beneath clubs
with Christmas lights for docks.
Illuminated masks flash over what little is visible of two divers—
a green flash of shoulder. a head peppered with a few shadows.

The image of a night diver's head rising from water
is an introvert's extravagance.
Isn't introspection extravagant? It's seeing extravagance
without being changed in the light that other people give off
as they gesticulate—that's the trick, that's what each of us has to beat.

We can't help seeping back into the palimpsests of our pasts,
into the way we wish we had lived these lives
that stare up at us from soup,
into the way we have of just plain living with the depths
too repressed not to be a part of our breathing, a pain we've grown used to
and call it "breath" if we can let the words form on our lips
before we give them away, before we lay ourselves open to stratagems,
ones we should have guessed at, given time's intricate diorama—
a thousand identical ships with red sails, lacquered red, closing in—
given the post-it-note on the refrigerator as wide as Mount Rushmore,
its large block letters to assist the aging Memory,
which is the lonely stepsister to Imagination, in any case, isn't it?

The two men in wet suits are drunk off their asses—
what they imagine they are saying is embarrassingly close.
One of them seems all the glaze of light off his glasses.
He's saying how it was when he left his body in Emergency.

I saw an orderly slip on a spot of blood, my blood,
and then the room went black, then white, and I was dead.
There were a number of shapes that seemed familiar
though the faces and names floated in a kindly ozone
that wouldn't let me match up face with shape. And besides,
all these figures milled around as if they were waiting
at a train station and too many hours had already passed
not to move around, stretch the legs, cover a yawn
as it blossomed on the face like an Asiatic lily.

The other man takes a gulp from a drink
as if he'd not been listening.
The bus could take us as far as the bridge blown down in the storm,
the bridge still a mess these many months after.
Most of us proceeded on foot, down one embankment and up the other.
By us I mean the group of strangers who'd become chummy
on the bus ride north from Monterrey
where the bus fumes are all these little flecks in the air,
black droplets of fog suspended there, you know, above the more immediate.
We drank Joya sodas and ate enchiladas on the Mexican side
in a tacqueria within sight of the concrete palisades
where all we tourists would soon identify ourselves
to reenter our workaday lives. The sun was multiplied all over the concrete.
The man next to me starts speaking out of the blue
about an Italian movie in which the protagonist drives deeper
into the woods, the ground covered with two or three inches of snow.
The protagonist has left the safety of his car, which, for some cinematic convenience,
won't start, won't budge. He's running where the cover isn't thick enough.
The land with its trees forms a bowl, an area where his shoulders can hunch up
as the bullet catches him, from behind, near the wing for his arm
which contorts like a spent firecracker as he collapses——
a close-up on the side of his body, the groove of his belt squirming a little.

St. Vitus' Dance, Teaching Hospital

*It would be good to give much thought, before
you try to find words for something so lost,...*
                                        —*R.M. Rilke*

We should think twice before we unpeel
childhood's humiliating documentary reel,
its delicate cellophane sticking to the wrist.

The glue on a plastic model Buick smears,
a heart murmur's imperceptible hand tremor.
The old doctor consistently hears my heart

murmuring Gaelic tropes, intermittent drifts
in the metronomic tilt, as if sharing his gift
he has to detect nothing's glitch on the disc

of his stethoscope. My thin arm bent back
to trigger some lever on my neck, I escape
and the moonlight-slatted ward rears close

at the juncture of flesh-fleck and nerve-sick
where fingers from the dark offer a paper cup,
its timely sweet sip I can't gulp fast enough.

Deserts and Oceans

Maybe R. can start from scratch. There is a lot of it, pink nose-hairs from the eraser nub that childhood lends each child, the shavings and broken pencil tips. Maybe he needs someone to count him off the way a stage manager, subtracting fingers, cues a newscaster, silence and then the words begin.

Is it the ancient Nepalese who depict the earth on the carapace of a giant tortoise in a green sun-drenched ocean depth? Is consciousness a termite palace someone else discovers, pulling back the floorboard with a crowbar?

R. will throw good money after bad because he's not sure he can trust his desire or the pride inside it. What he wants rubs his skin raw without redress.

Are there words for what the past would never give? He goes back into it, light redressing dirt and rock. When he thrashed his hand through a paloverde and blood welled from the cuts, he knew this act and its masochistic consequence were what people usually call memory's work.

The end of romance comes back like this, intermittently, and with a smell he's always thought was sage dried by winds traveling over dirt and rock. But people have corrected him over the years, saying, no, the distinct desert smell is creosote.

So maybe the lithe adventurer in the convertible beneath the palm trees was someone else, a person he watched down the slanted cement floor of some movie house, a figure that never really existed.

Wellfleet

He doesn't think the riptide will drag him out to deeper water. He thinks about lighthouses and marinas, about the glints when the sunlight touches every separate dip and swell.

Like tigers accustomed to their keepers, the waves lick his knees. He doesn't make any sudden movements.

Montreal Poem

So accustomed to snow falling from this busted gloaming,
trucks haul the accumulations to dump them in the river,
or to specially assigned "open spaces,"
or facilities specifically built to sluice snow through spouts

backing up at drains thick with suds. So much effort
to keep the sidewalks clear, to keep things moving.
In the museum, black patches punctuate white oiled surfaces,
life smudging through the daunting unintentions

to quiet us for good. If I could let the world go to pieces,
would the buzzards let cars scare them off their roadkill?
A cougar sits improbably astride a bronze bareback horse,
paws curling in, claws extended. This sculpture

must stand for something, it might as well be *fierceness,*
whatever wards off cravings for fame or food.
When I was younger, things came to me all at once,
no appetites waiting for permission in the vestibule.

I guess I should blame the alchemists for this limitlessness
as if each notion assumes a shape we must make room for,
the astrolabe with its garrulous parrot, the standing globe.
Do I need people to exceed themselves like puffs of smoke?

Outside, sub-zero plumes rise from the car exhausts.
Now that I'm older, *forever* is a morning song.
The sparrows, the juncos, all the little small birds, track the snow
in the spirit of Ornette Coleman, each horn precisely out of tune.

What exactly takes us as far as we can?
Is it fear crystallizing a pattern on the glass?
Who would have thought that it could feel this way, this orienting,
shoulder blades sharp, brain like dandelion fluff, four cardinal directions?

Bird Phonetics and Jazz Scat

The harvest will be grueling as in Breughel's work,
a man spun down on one knee, the flax cut just so far.
What remains to be cut looks like a giant with a butch,
that variation on the whiffle you received as a boy,
a stick of gunk pushing a phalanx of hair up in front.

Everybody was hardy back then—stoic silence a virtue.
But there's the feeling that something has gotten away,
some bottle flute you might have held, a shard of glass.
How can the present be decadent? There's so little of it.
The trombone's cumbersome slide sharpens its spare use.

The blackbirds can scatter as much seed as they consume,
absorb all other colors beneath their wings. They even sing
on certain nights, a bare sweet minimal skill, not censured
silent compliance. If scarcity were true, the wood-peewee
couldn't sing his name, three *pee-ah-wee's*, then a *wee-ooo*.

Doxology to scatology, we were meant to try every tone.
Else God, bored with the woods, would take back his gifts,
clouds of manna, loaves and fishes, even the widow's thrift.
Luck rejects all points of view, and only then does motion
become agility and stealth. Expectancy scars every nerve

out to the edge of the black river where no fruit is forbidden.
Silence evaporates, gone up ahead as airy as death's touch.
Sweet-sweet, chew-chew, then a thin sharp *spit*. Hear that.
The indigo bunting chooses you, it exudes its own empirics
beyond the body proper and improper, all the trajectories,

the whole biological effort, especially the singing, especially
the night singing when it wouldn't be habitual, no barricades
nor fortresses, no endings nor beginnings. You are certain
if some unkind fate befell the bird, its color would sing in you
a few syllables, the oracular whisper of mountains and caves.

To Cesare Pavese from the Shores of the Mississippi

Whether you're watching the movie star
with a Chianti bottle looped on her finger
as she pays for a basket of olives
or you're eyeing the fishing boats at sea,
whether your notion of love forgives
or condemns every last man to desire,
I talk to you, dead by pills or pistol
or, dead like the drunks in your poems,
freefalling the terraces above the sea,
a rock or a root opening your brain
and letting your lungs fill with salt.
Maybe we share the same disease,
the same twisted scarcity, the same lips.

The way I see it: you took your life
so mine might start,
give or take a few moments,
as processes like transmigration take,
given how the human spark
somersaults one soul to the next.
I've endured the eroding murmurs
because I barely hear them.
Maybe they're the narcissism
I've told myself I hate.
I never said I was a genius.
I never said I was patient.
How does forgiveness work?

You and I crave the light of women
along hotel corridors,
past the statues of soldiers,
past pigeons we don't mean to kick,
the birds' iridescent throats
softly moaning, as if lifting everything.
I want to cry my people, my people,
but they're cut in half by this river
drowning the fool who dunks his head.

Close to the bluff the city's named for,
the Chickasaws hauled dirt from somewhere
to raise this grave mound
so their dead might look down on the river and live.

I carry a coin the color of coffee with a little milk,
a lire coin I saved from a bootblack,
wet hair slicked back,
a grimace around his eyes and mouth,
your spitting image.
Should I apologize for what I want?
Maybe death is not the other side of hunger.
Without desires, aren't we dirt?
This is how lights pass over barges at night.
Mosquitoes rise for swooping bats.
It's our lot to hug shadows:
the way you wrote this, I believe
these embraces, like rain, quicken the vines and dirt.

Repent or Perish

I

I wish someone would pay a little attention to what
my records will never register. I'm reconsidering
the deadliness of the sins: pride, wrath, envy.
I can never recite them all: the palms of the hands
press into a pinecone, all one body—at least that's
what the Buddhists say and probably the Taoists too
though the words slip into invisibility,
which has its own several forms
though our lexicon can't draw the coastline,
never mind the vague circumference. I get like this
every time I remember the graffiti in Oklahoma City
chalked on a low cement hedge, Lisa and I headed out
for Chinese, her a mound of rice and me tangerine beef.
Repent or perish, repent or perish, repent or perish.
The smugness makes me a little crazy, a little rabid,
a poisonous foam through teeth. Why don't they admit
I'm just like them, a body that will burn like a leaf?

Some religions call it "a wake," some "a homegoing,"
some "a showing." I call it tardy, the act of trying
to catch a friend on the platform after the train has left.
I stand above my own eyes and whisper: Dear cousin,
I died while you were cutting a peach onto corn flakes.
I died when every woman I ever loved said
we couldn't see each other. I remember the thorns
in the paloverde, how I thrashed my palm
through branches I presumed were soft as mimosa,
the unsheathed claws of a nine-month-old feral cat.
I'm looking back now all the time, the act I swore
I'd never do. I'm looking back as the harbor recedes,
the moored boats and, further back, lobster traps
piled up or toppling down like Egyptian obelisks.
Pride says good riddance, envy clutching the air.
Women's bodies are hunkered down in armchairs,
the anger crumbling like an old block of cheese.

There is no place to lie down and curl up on this boat,
what with the miles of thick rope and the pitching
of the deck. Please excuse my stare. I'd like to say
my eyes don't stop going out, nothing stopping sight
from flying further and further out, sky and water.

2

I confess I feel disarmed late at night in men's rooms,
not the kind so snooty to hire an attendant, but those
with the scented disinfectant nearly evaporated
way after midnight as I tip toward the urinal,
my fly finally undone, my fingers fumbling.
I close my eyes and press my forehead to a cool patch
of tile, the patch of brain pressing back, a pause and then
the first hard drill of pee on porcelain, then dribbling
off and on till my brain begins to reassemble the hum
above the chatter, the larger sound, what the ancients
called music, how some nights we don't hear the insects
vibrating their armor though they whine like the births
of thousands of crying Toms, Dicks, and Harrys.
I call one of them Possum because its white face
and pointed teeth sustain a ruthless honesty.
It braces itself, its mouth agape, a hiss from its throat.
It is hunger, it is breath. Every time I remember,
it's a flash at my feet. I'm reconsidering a pattern
that used to dominate my way of thinking, but I've
finally relented, the way the blue heron works his wings
as if reluctantly rising, regret lifting into elation.

When I cut my heel up breaking in a pair of shoes,
I let myself drag the bum foot behind me,
feeling older than my years, glaring at pitying stares
or curt silence as I pass people talking on the sidewalk.
The only way I can cry is to clutch a possum at my throat,
taste the drool on its fur. The only way I can cry
is to lop the yellow heads off weeds with a scythe
or look out the window, poles whizzing across it
as the bullet train reaches dizzying speed. The truth is
I took one punch. Doyle, out of prison three days,
shoved his knuckles in my face, once, as if a form
of etiquette, really—he seemed hesitant about it.
I had just called him a junkie after he heaved a knife
from two blocks away. He assumed I had slighted him,
using some ancient code, some clan loyalty.

I haven't seen Doyle in years, may his face rot
with the glow from the very best dope. He once
asked me to share the front seat of a stolen 'Vette.
He once asked me to share a dripping needle.
I'm probably not giving him his due—maybe
he became a man of the cloth late in life
after numerous run-ins with the arbitrary limits
we call the law. That's why shrinks are sorcerers
and sane people fear them, isn't it? It's the poets
I owe my life to, Keats and Catullus, Lenny Bruce too,
that pistol. He tested the patience of them all.
When I talk, it's Walt jabbering with Hart Crane
if anyone can stand to read a well-thumbed phone book
and then watch people's faces pass like sailboats,
various eyebrows, different noses, the six million
glorious names in Rome, Asian and African mouths
boisterously speaking Italian in the slum near the trains.
I'm trying to hold my tongue as much as possible.
I'm trying to stop parsing white from off-white,
cobalt from indigo. I'm on my way. I could never hate
my own miserable body. Draw a circle around me,
and I'll swerve around like an injured dog, a bird
dipping between one coiffed wind and the next. Soon
the brain will let my femur rumble with dirt beetles.
For now, I'll flex my fingers and shake them, shake them out.

Notes

Page 13   The opening of "'I Begin" is from *The Diaries of Paul Klee, 1898-1918,* University of California Press, 1964.

Page 14   "Paradise is not your milieu" in "Morning and Night" is a paraphrase from Frank O'Hara's poem "Fond Sonore." His original goes

I think that it would be nice to go away
but that's reserved for TV and who wants to end up in Paradise
it's not our milieu
we would be lost as a fish is lost when it has to swim

Page 17   The title "Cousins of the Heart" is an allusion to Nancy Eimers' poem "No Friends of the Heart" and is dedicated to her.

Page 26   ""Blues in Blueprint (Alternate Take)" borrows the original take's title from a Duke Ellington song. The second stanza briefly quotes Gerard Manly Hopkins' sonnet #69.

Pages 39, 40, 50   Three poems "Bluest Thing," "Mary Sends a Clipping of a Man Who Eats Stones," and "Health Care, Taoist Mysticism, and Voodoo" quote from a translation of the *Book of Lieh-tzu,* translator A. C. Graham, Columbia University Press, second edition, 1990.

Page 40   "Mary Sends a Clipping of a Man Who Eats Stones" is dedicated to Mary Ruefle.

Page 46   "Years after the Hurricane" uses "pop-outs" as a term for deer. I first heard this term in conversation with Nancy Eimers. I suspect the term is hers.

Page 58   "Art and Death" is dedicated to Bill Olsen.

Page 61   "Three Odd Ducks on the Atlantic" uses esoteric lore from *The Curious Lore of Gems.*

Page 63   "Two Studies of two Male Figures" is dedicated to Dave Theis. The poem pays homage to Francis Bacon's paintings and Bernardo Bertolucci's film *The Conformist.* The first stanza makes a brief allusion to a translation of Blaise Pascal's *Les Pensées.*

Page 65   "St. Vitus' Dance, Teaching Hospital" has a epigraph from Rainer Maria Rilke, *New Poems,* 1907, translator Edward Snow, North Point Press, 1990.

Page 70   "To Cesare Pavese on the Shores of the Mississippi" briefly quotes Pavese's letters.

Page 72   "Repent or Perish" is dedicated to Lisa Lewis and Dinah Cox.

—Megan Bean

Richard Lyons has taught literature and creative writing for more than two decades at Mississippi State University. Lyons is a former winner of the "Discovery" Award from *The Nation* and the 92nd Street YHMA in New York City and the Lavan Younger Poet's Prize from the chancellors of the Academy of American Poets in New York City. His other collections include *These Modern Nights, Hours of the Cardinal,* and *Fleur Carnivore.* Born in Boston, he hails from the Mid-South where he lives with his wife and his cats.